D1442994

Also by Jarlath Regan

HOW TO BREAK BAD NEWS

And published by Transworld Ireland

Jarlath Regan is an award-winning stand-up comedian and greeting-card maker. He spent much of his early life drawing representations of Michael Jackson with an over-sized head. In 1999 he was meant to attend Art College, but due to his careers guidance counsellor's inability to 'work the internet' he was forced to attend University College Dublin instead. It was there, while studying politics, that he was drawn to Tina Rowland's pixy head. They fell in love and were married in October 2009. Today they live in Dublin with their son Michael and together they are working on the next stage of their life.

Jarlath performs stand-up throughout the UK and Ireland and continues to sell his greeting cards through his website **www.jigser.com**

www.transworldireland.ie
www.**rbooks**.co.uk

Putting a Ring on It

What not to do when attempting to get married

Jarlath Regan

TRANSWORLD IRELAND

TRANSWORLD IRELAND
an imprint of The Random House Group Limited
20 Vauxhall Bridge Road, London SW1V 2SA
www.rbooks.co.uk

First published in 2011 by Transworld Ireland,
a division of Transworld Publishers

A CIP catalogue record for this book
is available from the British Library.

ISBN 9781848271081

Addresses for Random House Group Ltd companies outside the UK
can be found at: www.randomhouse.co.uk
The Random House Group Ltd Reg. No. 954009

The Random House Group Ltd supports the Forest Stewardship
Council (FSC), the leading international forest-certification organization. All our
titles that are printed on Greenpeace-approved FSC-certified paper carry the FSC logo.
Our paper procurement policy can be found at
www.rbooks.co.uk/environment

Typeset in Jd font
Printed and bound in Great Britain by
MPG Books Group

2 4 6 8 10 9 7 5 3 1

For my parents,
Tady and Maire Regan.

Acknowledgements

The book you are holding in your hands is a product of hard work, sweat, pride-swallowing, late nights and determination in the face of horrendously difficult circumstances. But enough about me and what I did, there are a lot of other people who deserve some thanks.

Firstly, there is Cormac O'Connor. Without this talented little devil this book would never have been made. Then there is the massive thank you I owe to Eoin and Jessica at Transworld for all their work, help and understanding during the very difficult period in which this book was written. After them I have to thank Lauren Hadden of Lisa Richards. Without Lauren there is no way this second book could have come about. Thanks for all your help, encouragement and support along the way.

Thanks also to my sister, Maeve Regan. Your friendship and advice helped to keep this book afloat and ultimately allowed it to keep its heart. Sincere thanks to Mick and Noreen Rowland, probably the most generous and loving people you could ever meet. This book owes more to your hospitality and generosity than you will ever fully know. Thanks also to my own parents, Tady and Maire, without whom I would have nothing. I hope you know how much I appreciate everything you have done for me and my family. Thanks, as always, to my big brother and sister, Adrian and Caragh, for always being there for me.

And finally to my wife, Tina. There is absolutely no way that this book would be here without you. You believed in it every step of the way – even when I didn't. This is your book as much as it is mine. I love you. And finally, thanks to the little baby Michael for making me realize what love truly means.

Introduction

Like most men, I had no idea what I was getting involved in when I first thought I'd like to marry the woman I love. I was flabbergasted that as soon as I told people we were engaged, they wanted to know when the wedding would take place. I had assumed there would be a period of time before people asked those kinds of questions. But it turns out that that period of time is about two seconds. I'm sure it makes many men's heads spin that within a week of putting a ring on it you're venue hunting, colour matching, flower picking, invitation designing and attending something I never knew existed – A Wedding Fair.

If you're a reasonably normal person it can all become too much and the light, love and humour can often become drained from the whole experience. Between the losing weight, the mounting costs, the guest list conundrums, the seating plan sketches, the swing band auditions, the prayers for good weather, and the need to 'get it done before the close of business', you consciously have to remind yourself to have fun. It seems odd, when you are constantly being advised on how things should be done, that fun is rarely part of the conversation.

That's the stupid thing about wedding advice, in my opinion. There is no right or wrong, there is only what's right for you. To me laughter and fun are what everyone wants on their wedding day. This is not a book of genuine advice but I hope it will bring you some fun. At the end of the day, that's always pretty useful.

Jarlath

Chapter 1:
The Proposal

Never to be referred to as
'my rush of blood to the head'.

Be sure to ask yourself, 'Why am I asking this woman to marry me?'

'She terrifies me!'
is as good a reason
as any.

Before you pop the question
you may have to get her
father's permission...

Or you might get lucky.

When asking for her father's permission do not prepare a good conversation starter...

Just wing it.

Create the proposal of her
dreams...

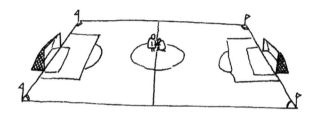

Not yours.

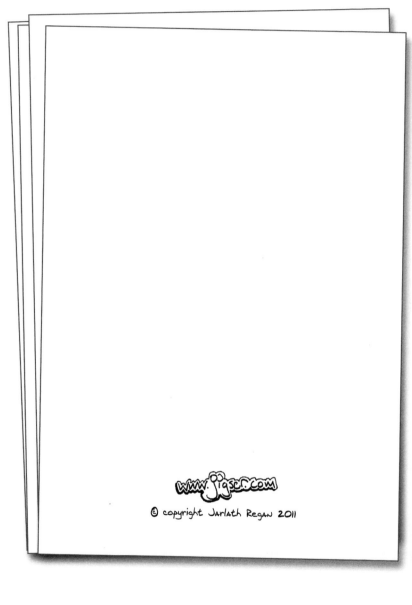

Make it a surprise...

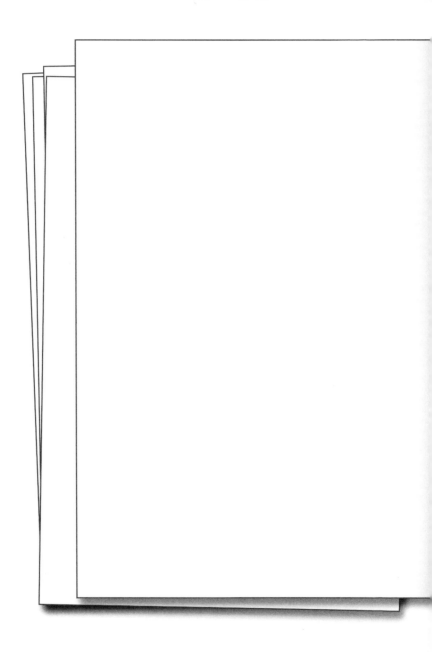

...but not too much of a
surprise.

The purpose of the proposal
is to find out if she wants to
marry you...

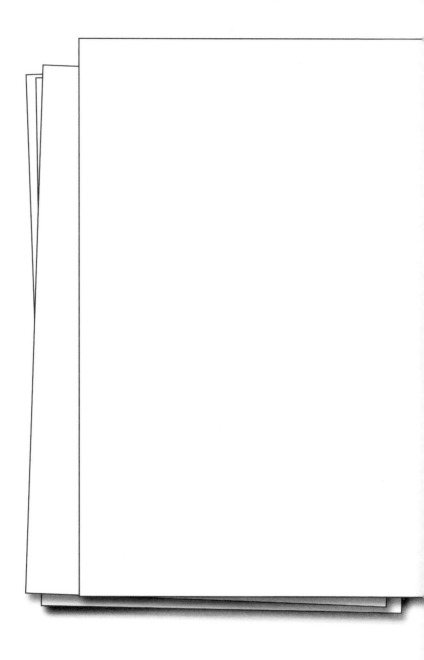

...not to make her say yes.

A successful proposal will probably
result in sex...

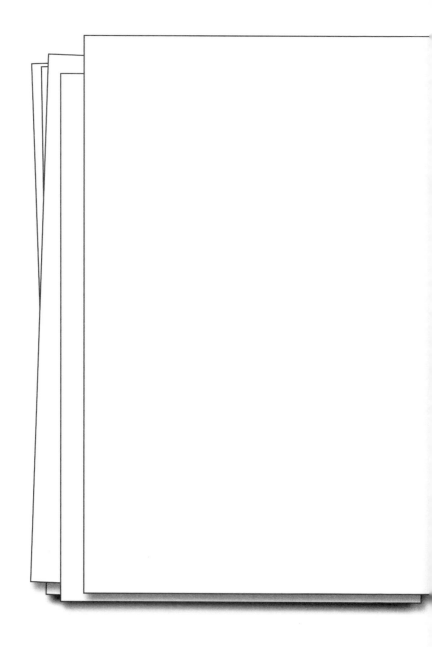

...but not immediately.

In the event of a refusal...

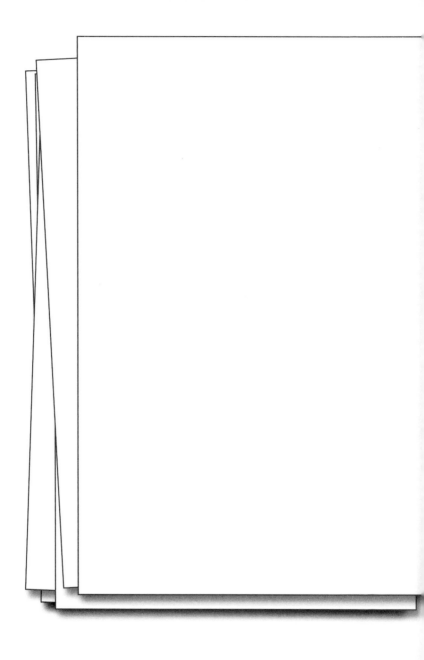

DO NOT PANIC.

Remember that the proposal will
either be the beginning...

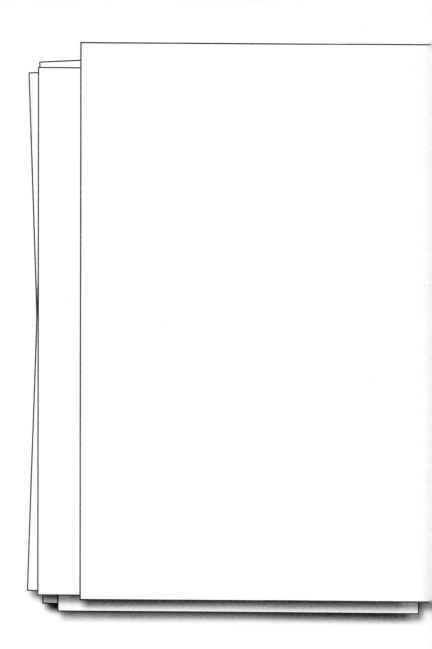

...or the end of the
relationship. Have an escape
route planned.

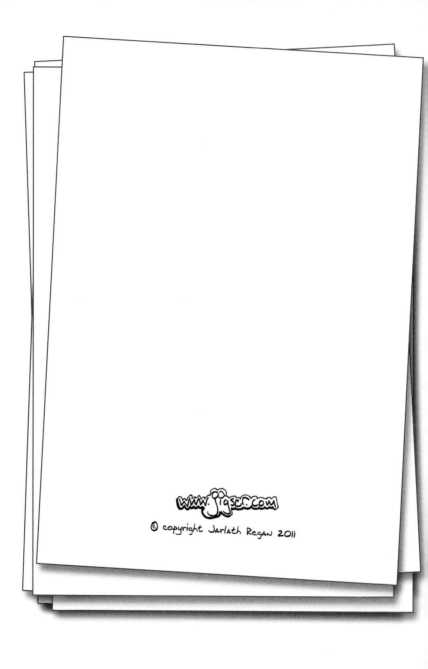

If she says no...

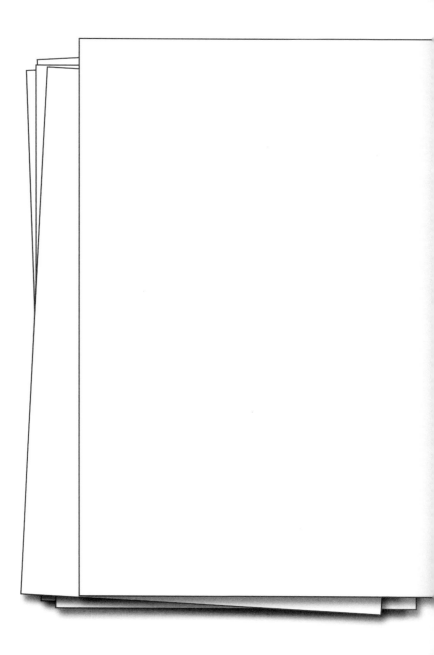

...try to maintain your dignity.

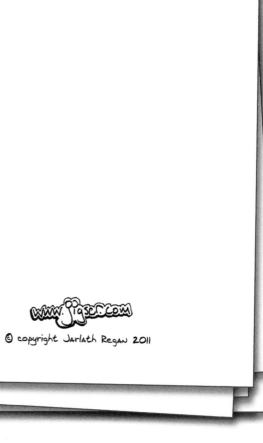

It's never too late to ask the question.

It may be more awkward but it's
never too late.

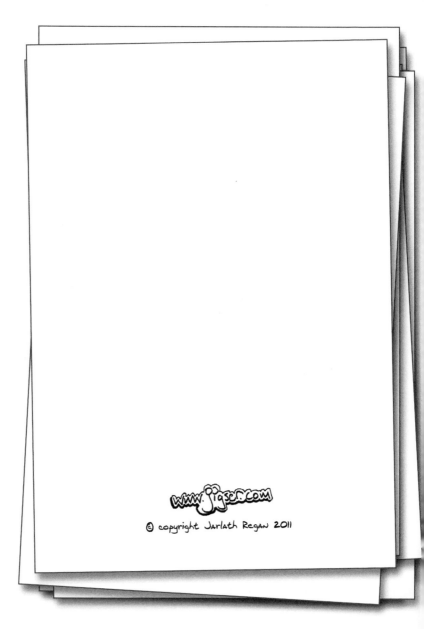

Chapter 2:
The Engagement

Never to be referred to as
'the stay of execution'.

Once you're engaged your
behaviour will have to change...

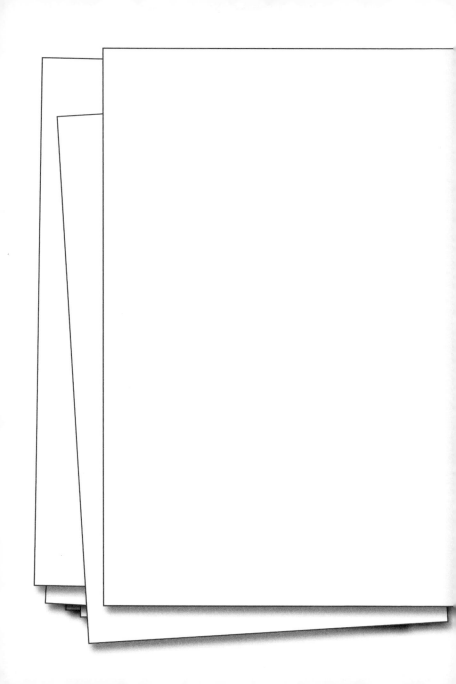

For one thing, you'll have
to stop having sex with
other people.

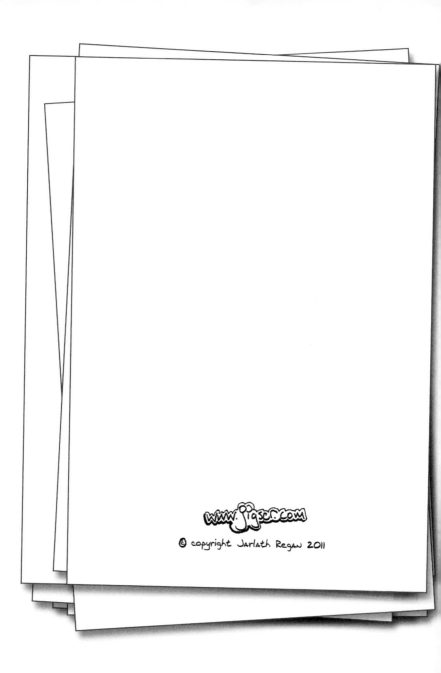

Her behaviour will definitely change as the day draws closer. Ignore most of it...

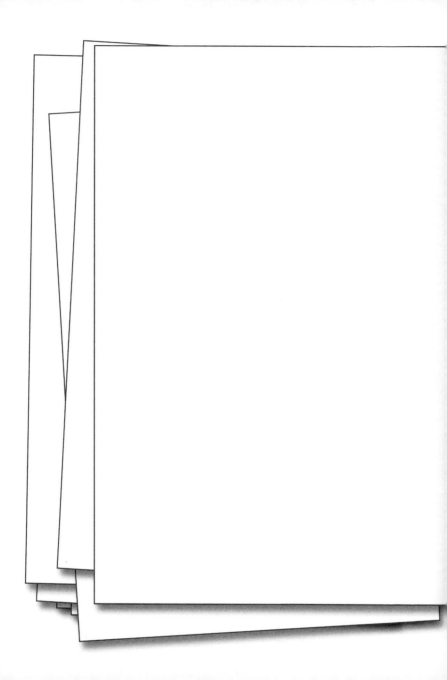

...but keep note of any weird shit that might be useful in future arguments.

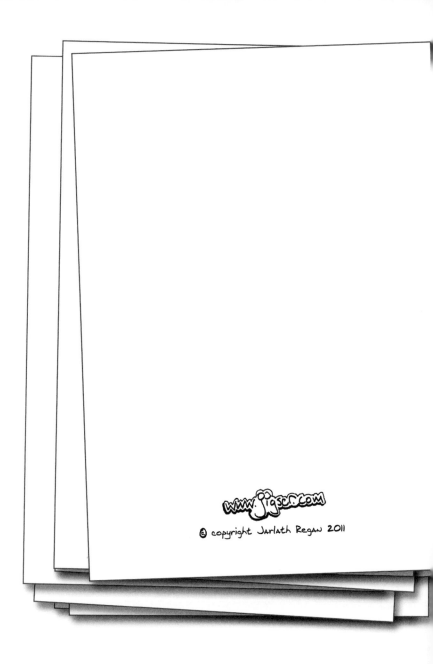

Encourage yourself to get in shape...

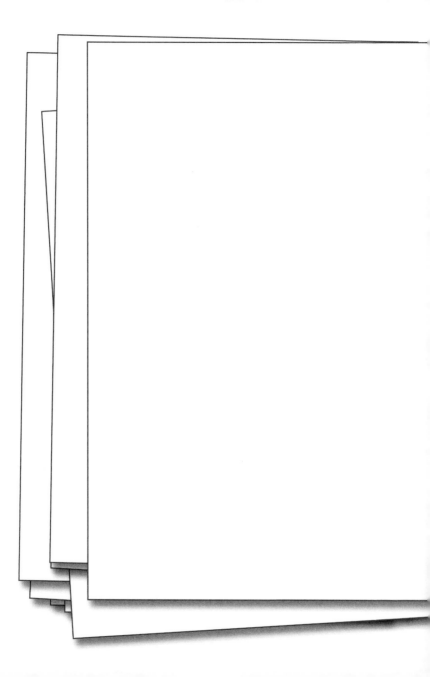

Do not encourage her.

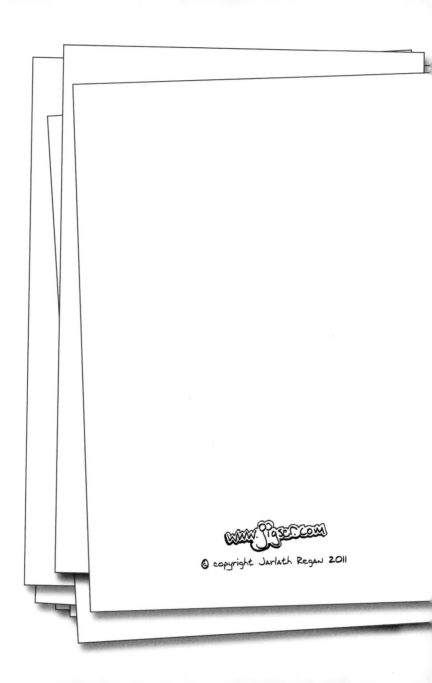

Buy her a gift for
her hen night...

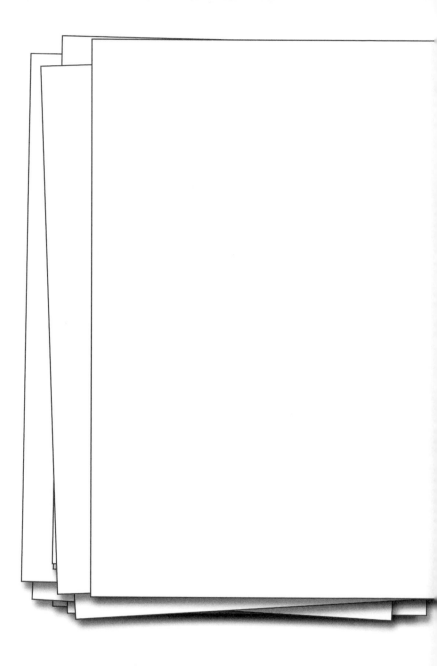

Something meaningful is
always best.

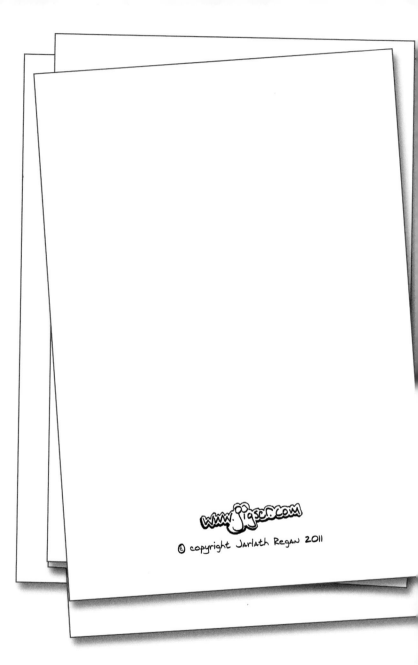

Tell your best man that you want a quiet stag night...

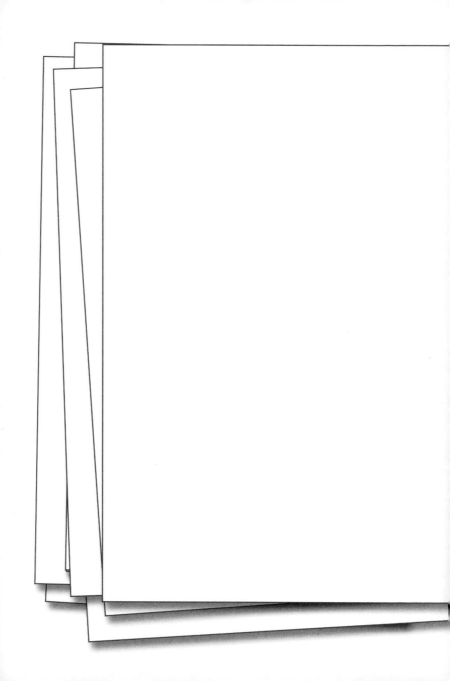

He will not listen.

Don't hold your stag do months
before the wedding...

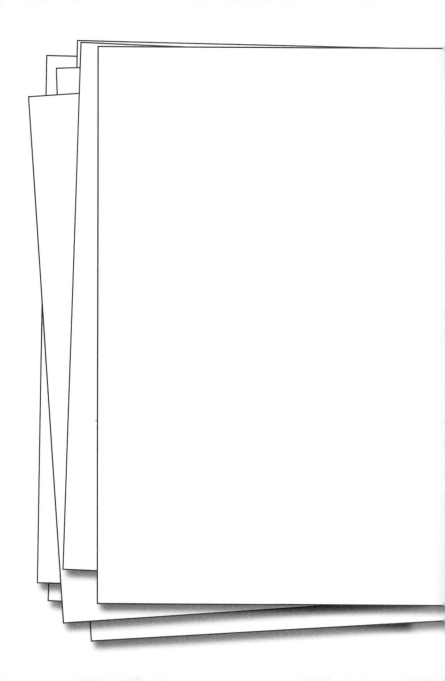

Hold it the night
before to make the ceremony
more entertaining.

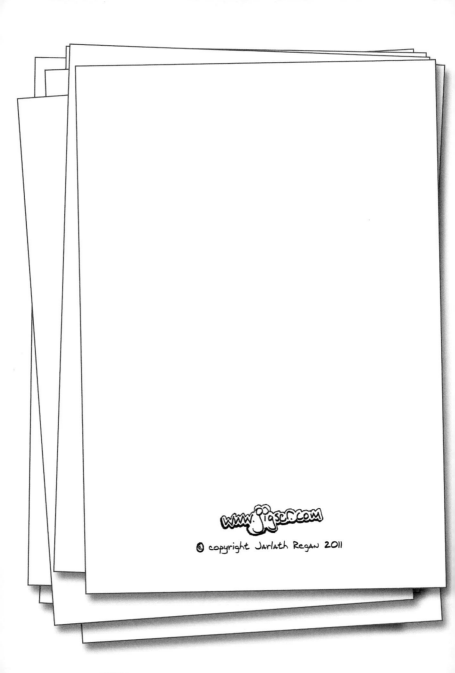

Treat her mother with total
contempt...

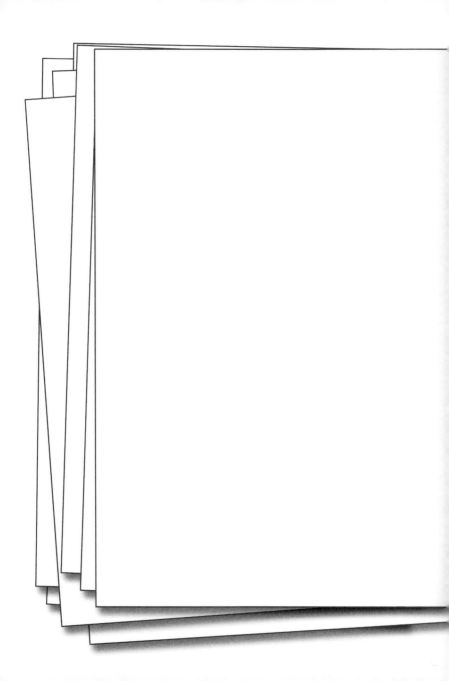

This will ensure that you have plenty of free time in years to come.

If her mother is being really
difficult, be patient...

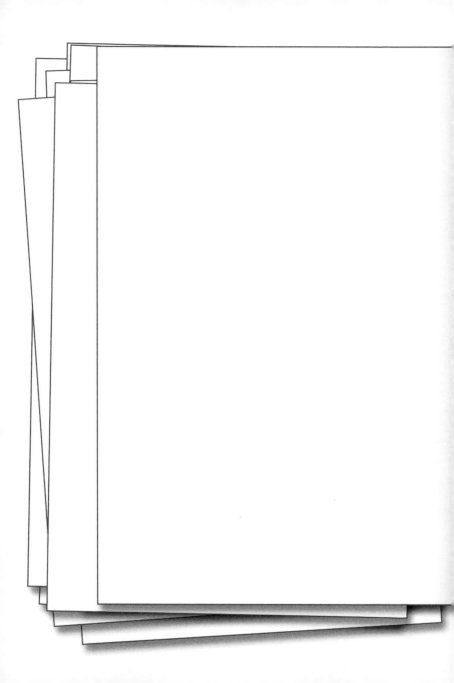

...and then have a friend run
her down in his car.

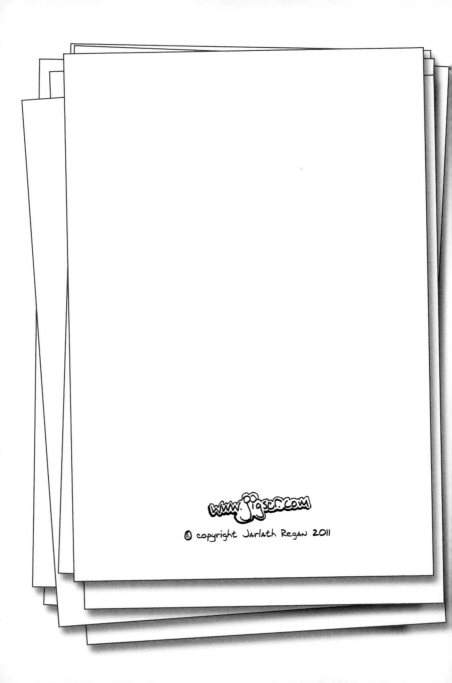

Tell your fiancée that if a sales person recommends she loses some weight, the appropriate response is...

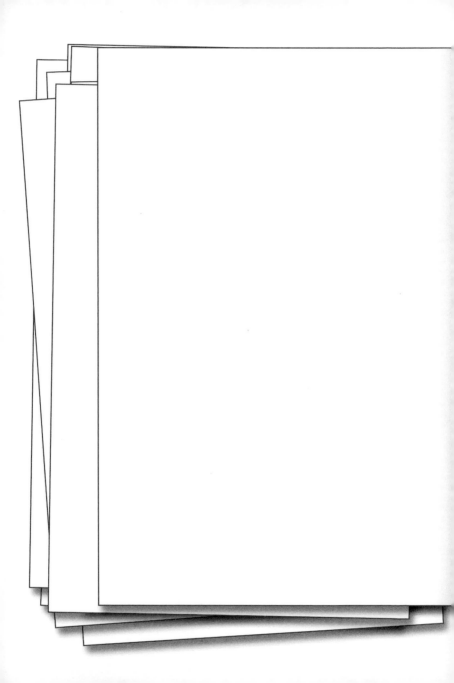

'I was going to ask you for some
tips, since you're clearly a
fat bitch.'

As the cost of the wedding
begins to add up...

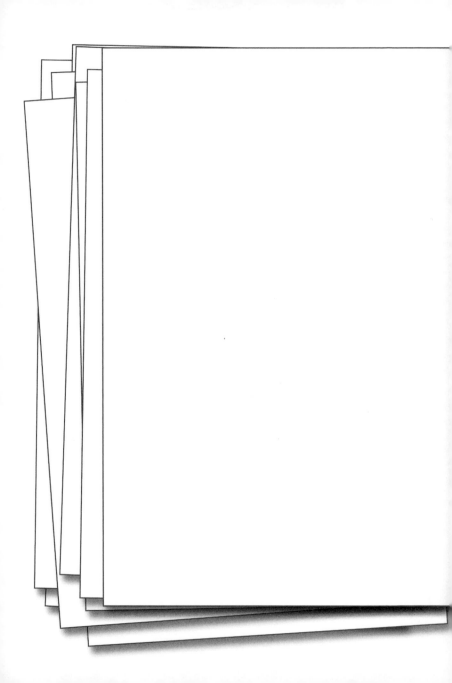

...you should explore new ways to generate income.

Remember that most hotels will
knock ten per cent off...

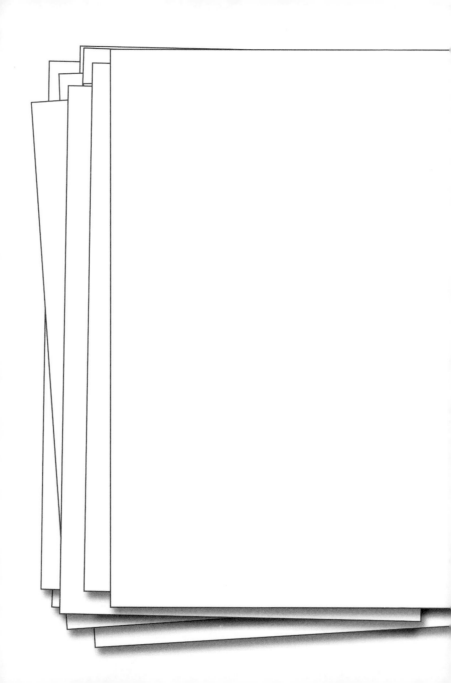

...if you pretend to be crippled.

Ever wondered which
aspects of the wedding are
her responsibility and which are
yours? Here's a simple guide...

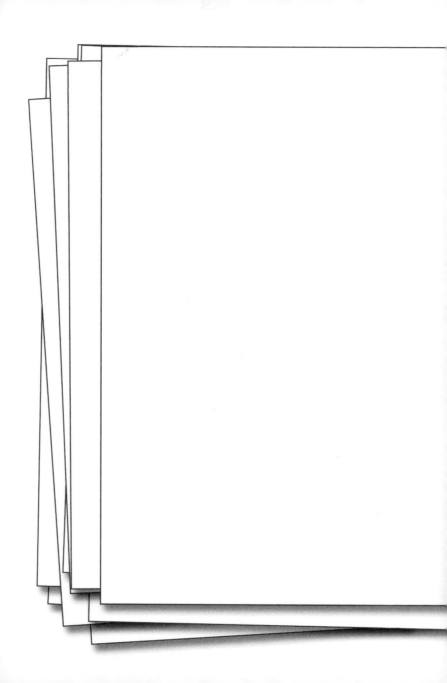

Things she gets worked up
about are hers. Things she
thinks you won't make a balls
of are yours.

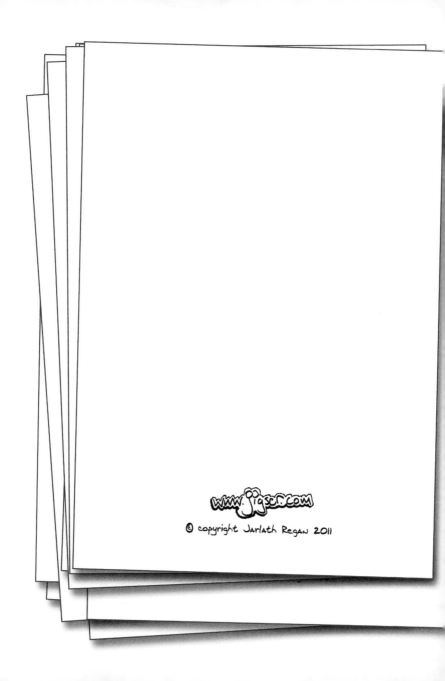

Still haven't heard from someone
you didn't really want to invite?
Worried that reminding them
could result in them actually
attending?

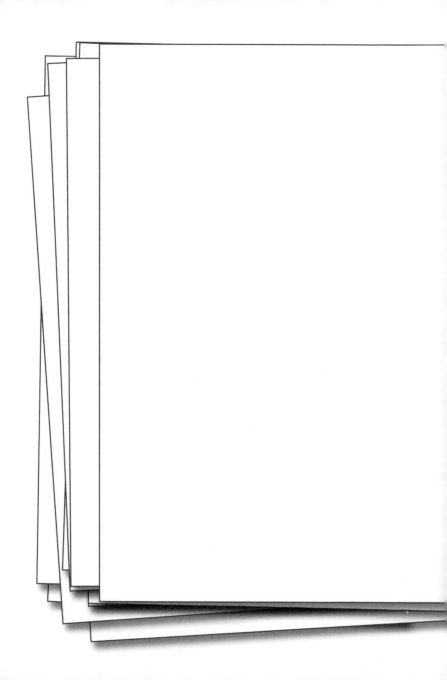

Try threatening their life with an anonymous crank call.

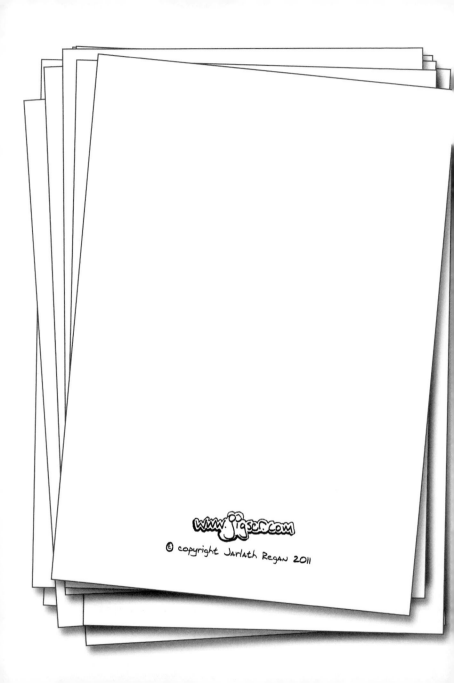

WANT to blow off some steam
the night before the wedding?

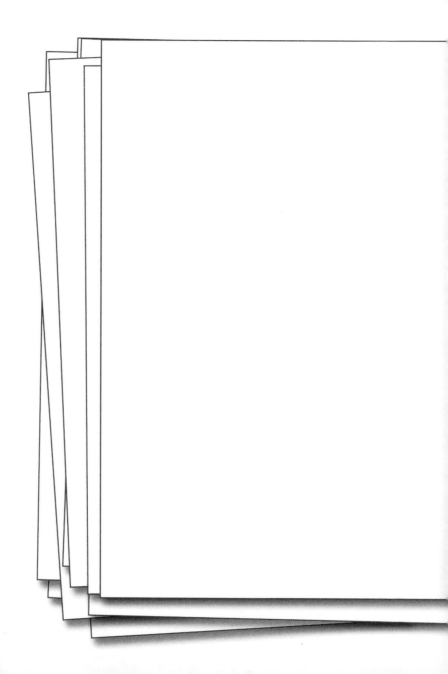

Inject yourself or one
of your groomsmen with some
Class A drugs.

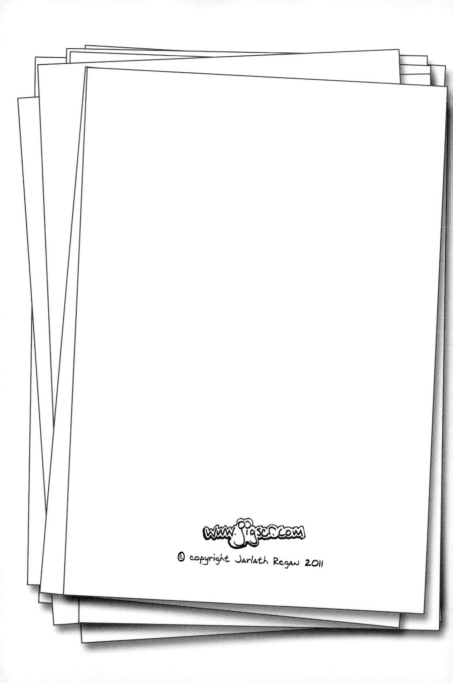

Being nervous the night before
is normal. Talk to your fiancée...

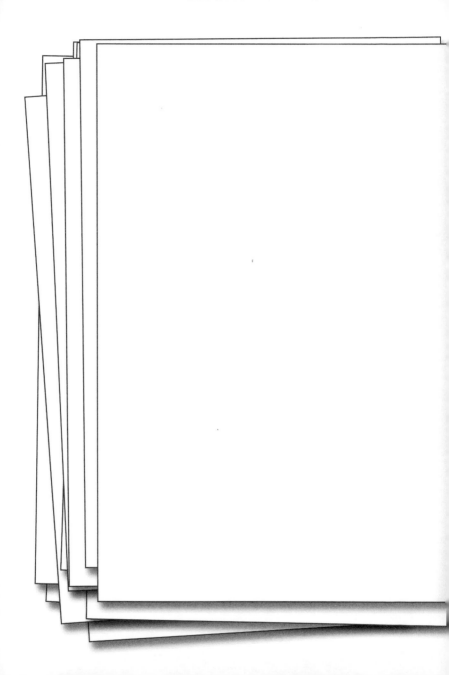

...or your travel agent.

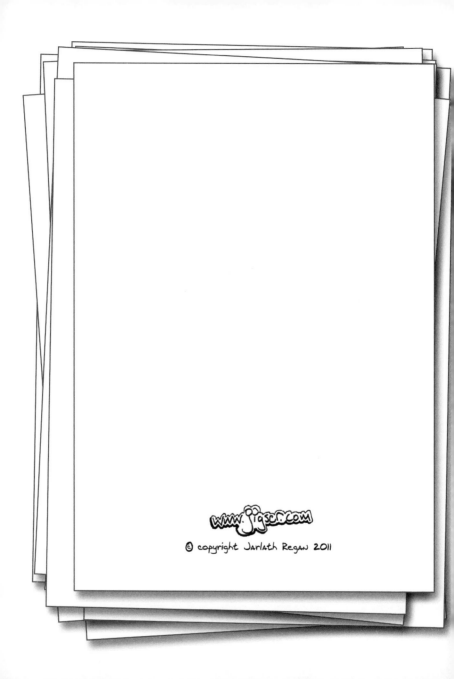

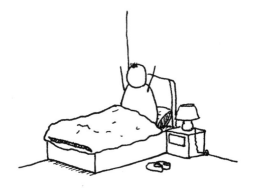

On the morning of the wedding...

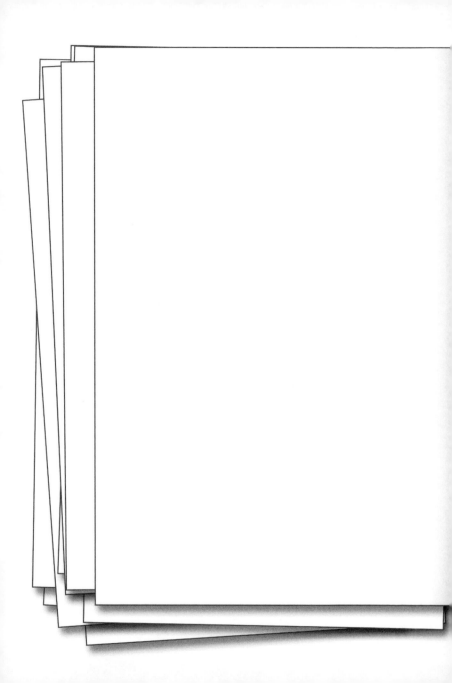

...stick to your normal
shaving routine.

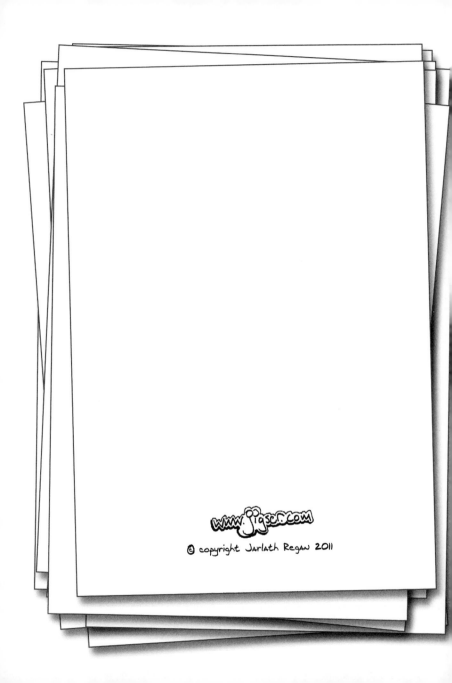

Be careful! Different flowers
have different meanings...

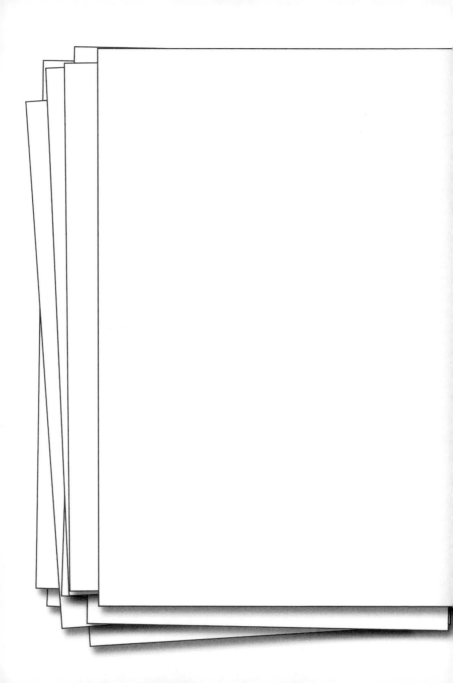

These ones mean, 'I am a cheapskate.'

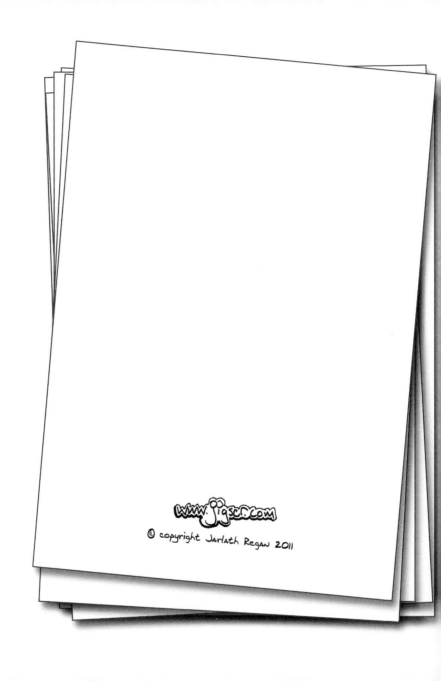

Chapter 3:
The Ceremony

Never to be referred to
as 'the day I ceased to exist'.

If you are thinking about not
showing up, remember...

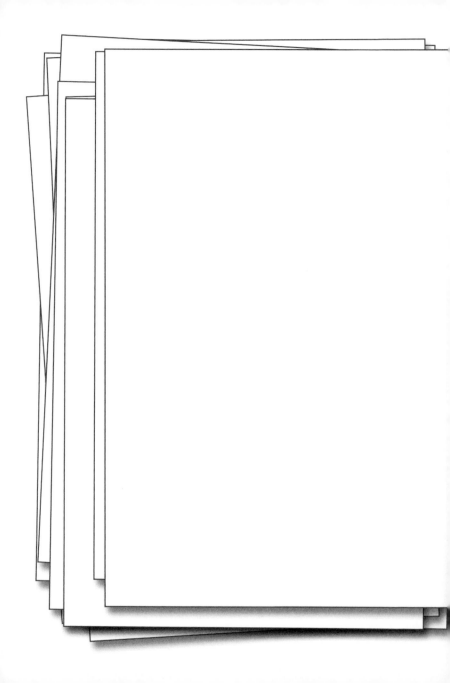

Cold feet are better than no feet.

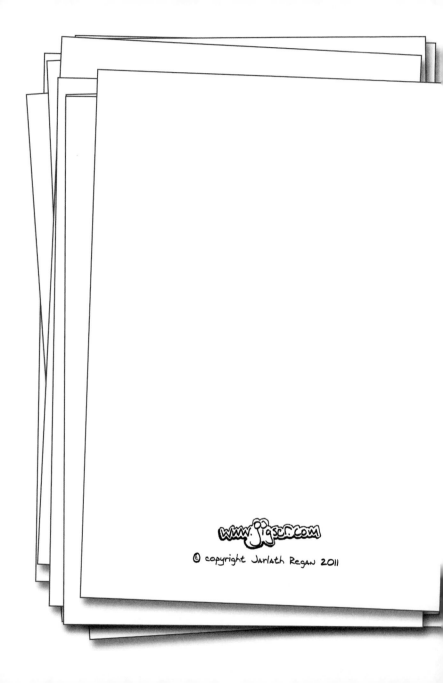

Being superstitious about the
wedding is a waste of time...

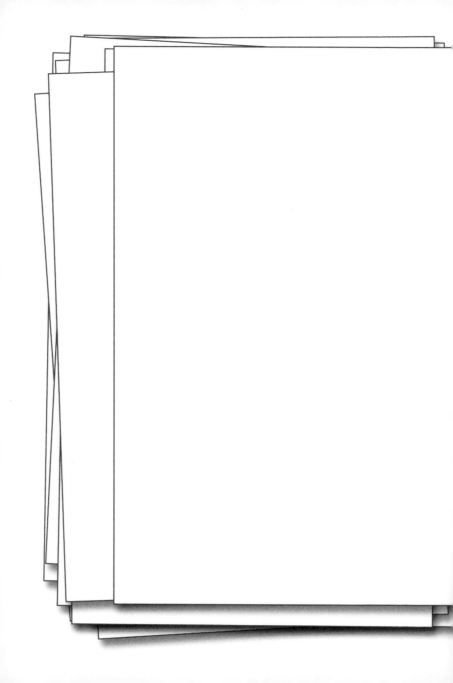

Pretty much everything
can be interpreted as good
or bad luck.

For the groom, punctuality on
the day is essential...

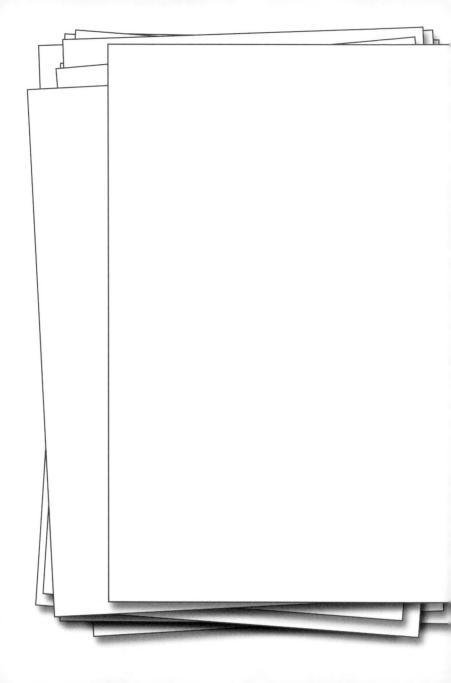

Smoking a cigarette before the
big event may calm your nerves...

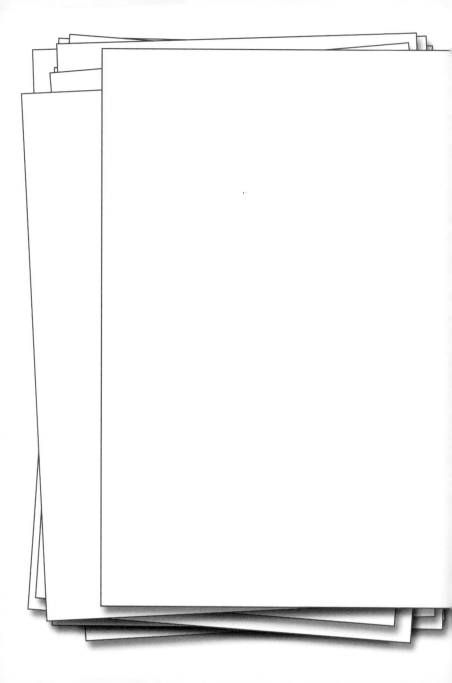

Smoking some crack will make
the ceremony difficult to
comprehend.

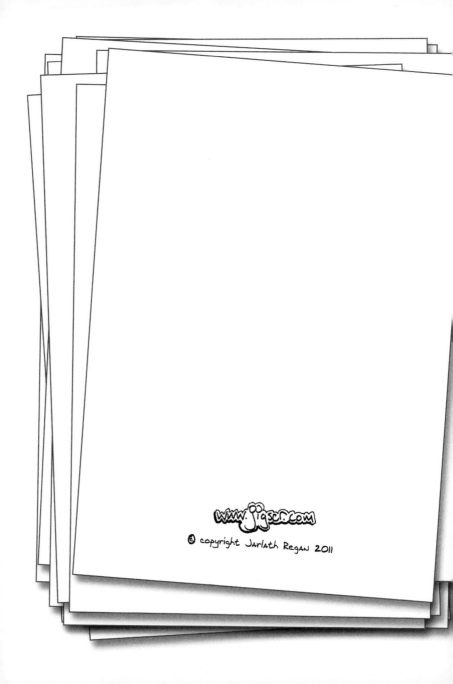

Some tears are OK...

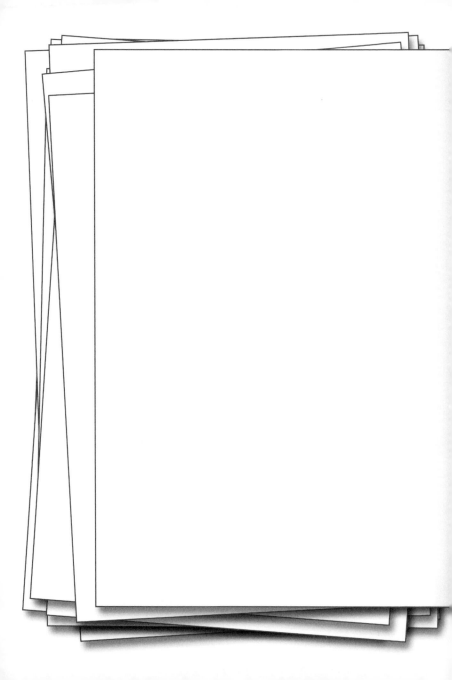

Some tears are not.

Impress your bride
by going the extra mile with
your appearance...

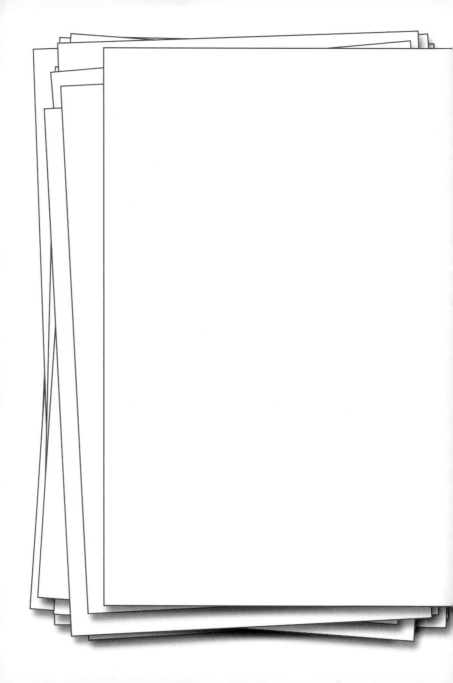

...but avoid clothes that could
be considered 'pimp-like'.

When your bride walks down
the aisle, never, ever, ever, ever,
ever, ever, ever...

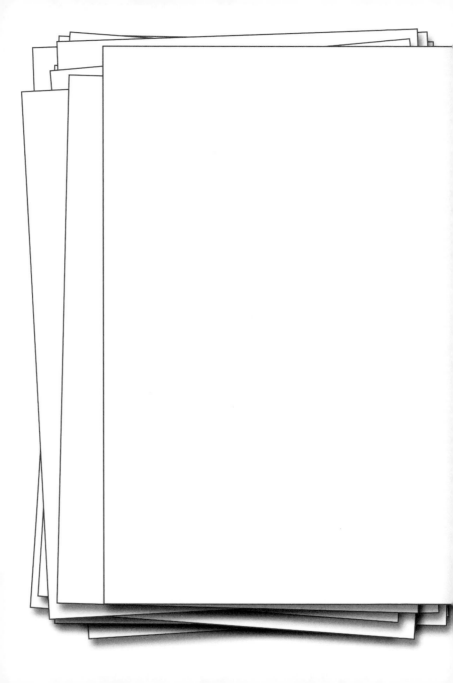

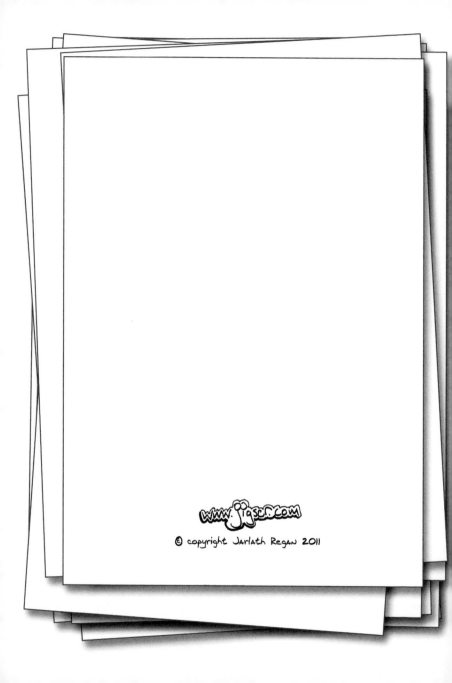

Your suit can be a lot
of things...

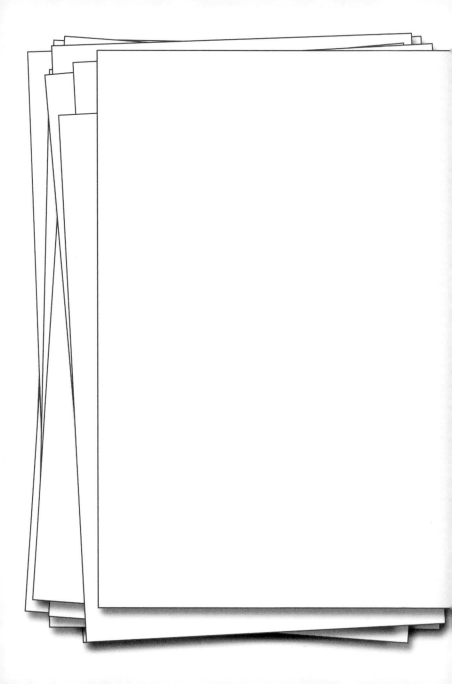

Tight is not one of them.

Things will go wrong on the day.
The main thing is...

...don't mention them
to her.

If her father tells you to take
good care of his daughter, the
appropriate response is...

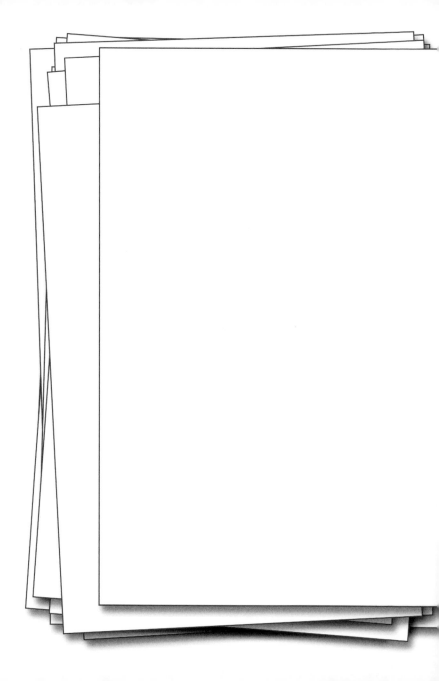

'With all due respect, she's not
your daughter any more.'

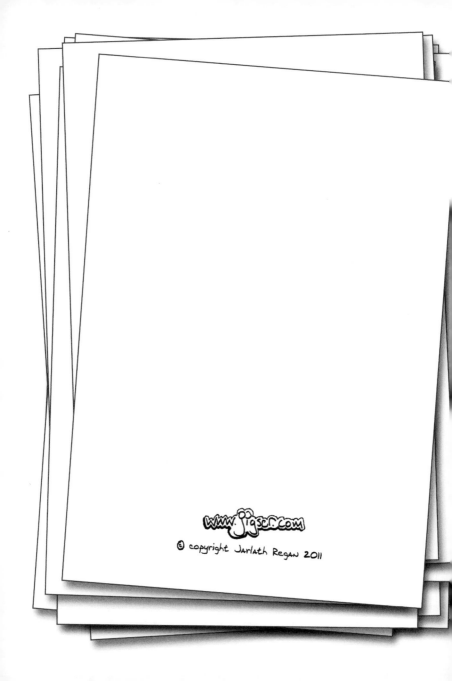

Be sure to ask the priest any
questions you may have...

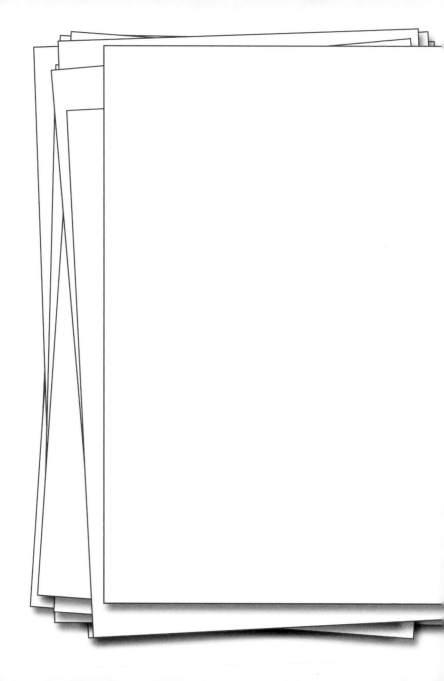

...before the ceremony.

Kiss your bride...

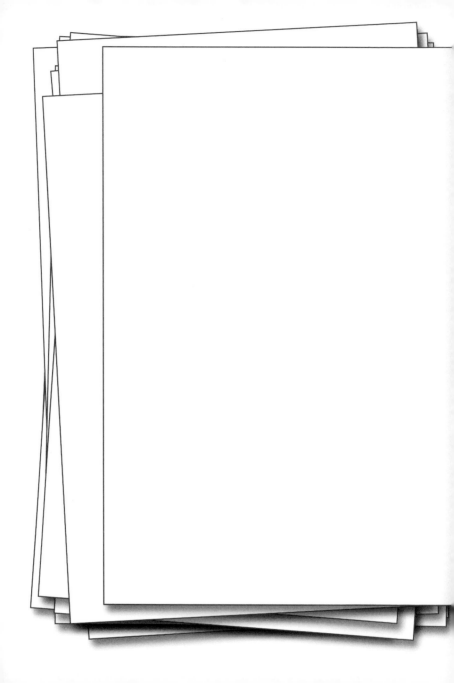

Don't face-fuck her.

Chapter 4:
The Reception

Never to be referred to as
'the piss-up afterwards'.

Some hotels will bend over
backwards for you...

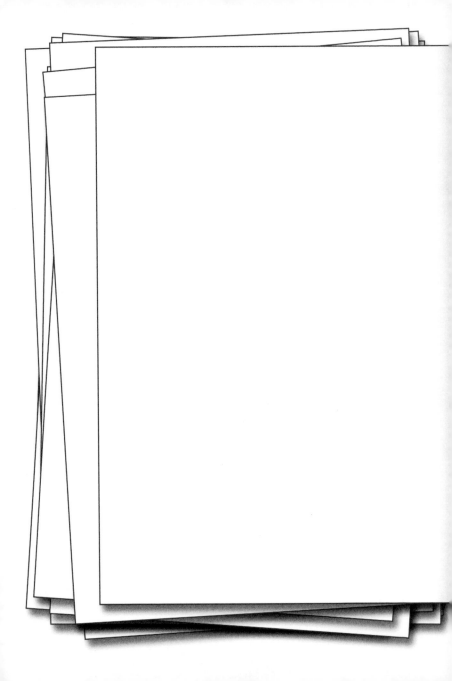

Some hotels will expect you to
bend over forwards
for them.

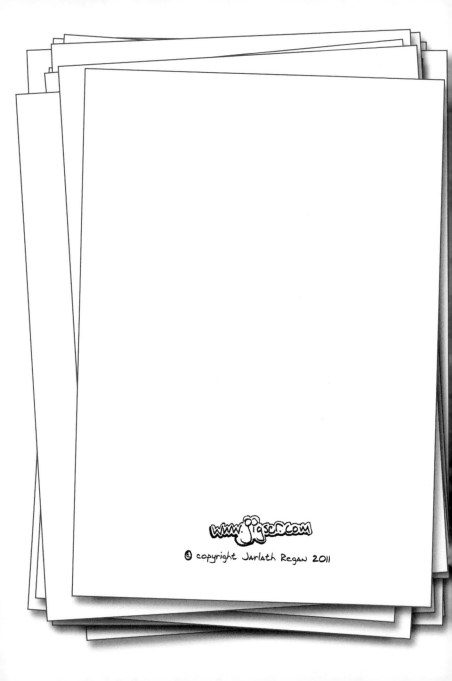

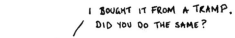

Save money on some things...

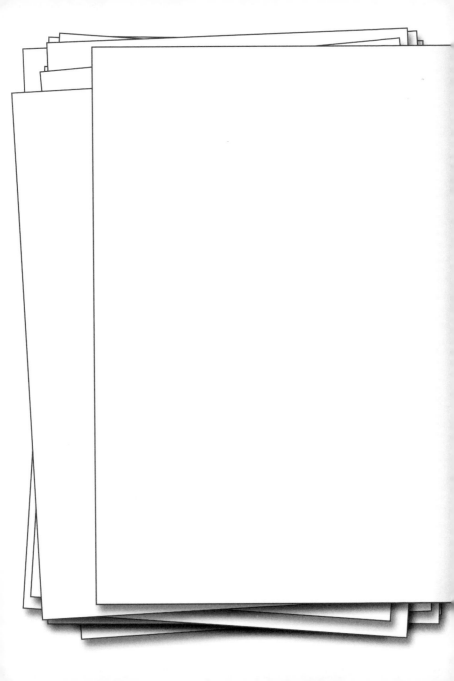

Be willing to spend
on other things.

When explaining to the
reception manager how important
this day is to you...

...don't hold back.

Some people consider it rude to write 'Cash Only Gifts' on the invitations...

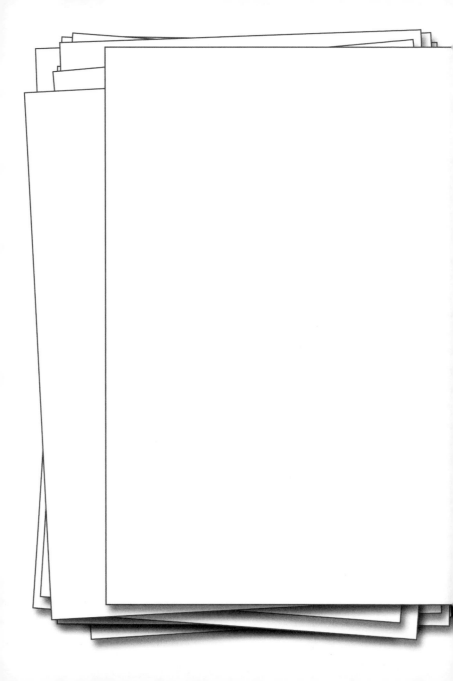

Don't invite these people.

You are not required to open
your gifts at the reception...

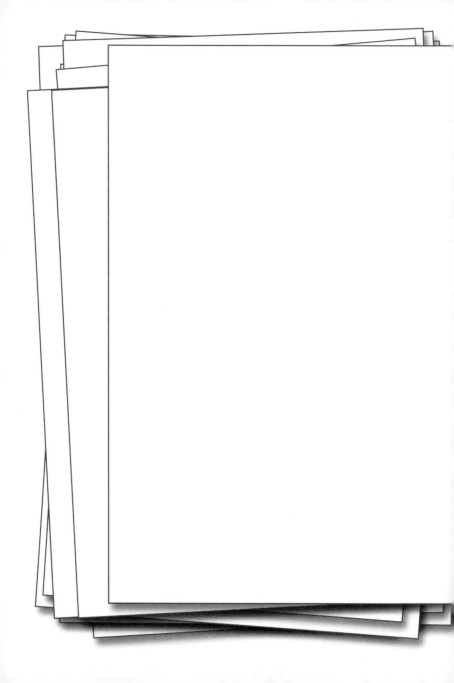

...unless otherwise directed.

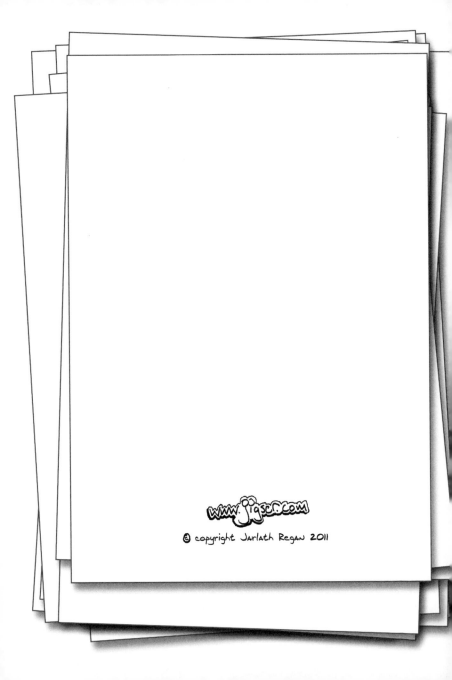

Worried about where to
sit that argumentative
relative or friend?

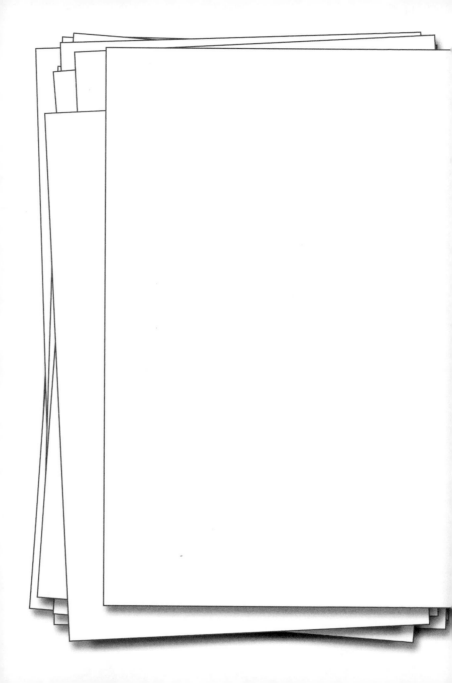

That's why God invented
the kiddies' table.

There are cheaper
alternatives to creating a
separate children's menu...

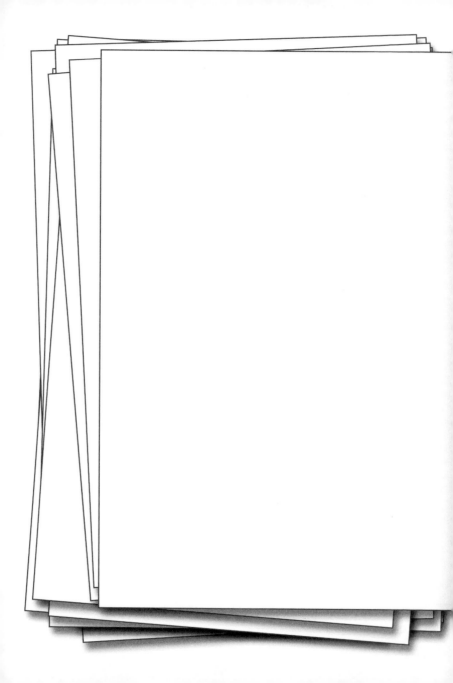

Slip a sleeping tablet into some
pop and allow your real guests
to relax.

Worried about what to feed guests with 'specific dietary requirements'?

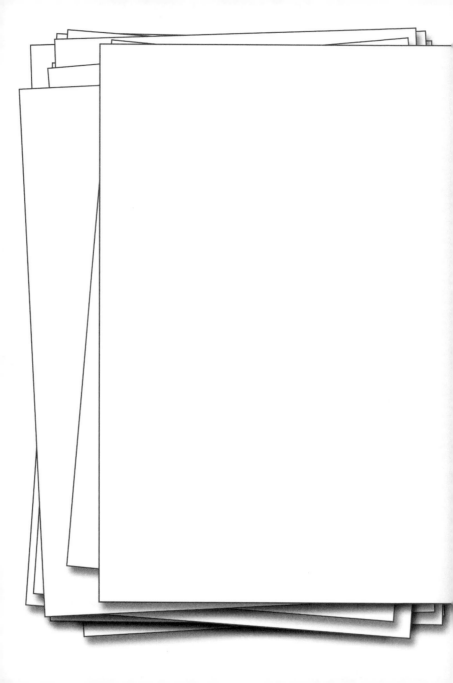

An emptied lawnmower bag
makes for a great vegetarian
main course.

Use your speech to say
the things you have always
wanted to say...

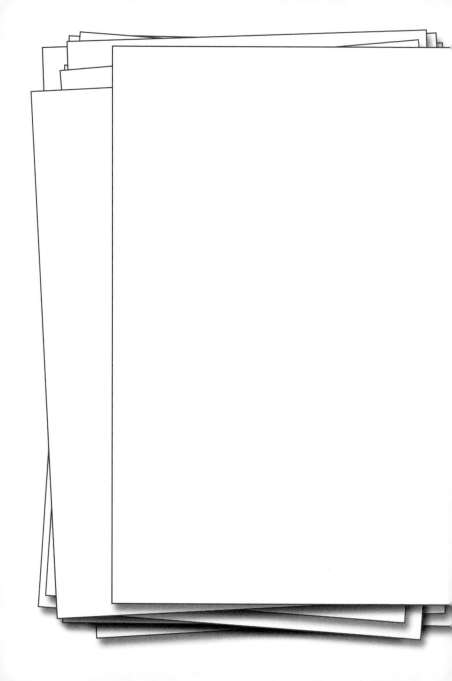

...rather than as a means to
settle old scores.

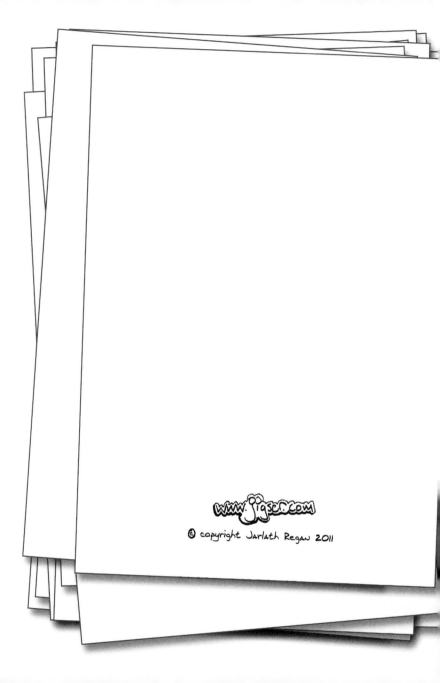

The number one reason
for writing a speech
which is complimentary to
your bride is...

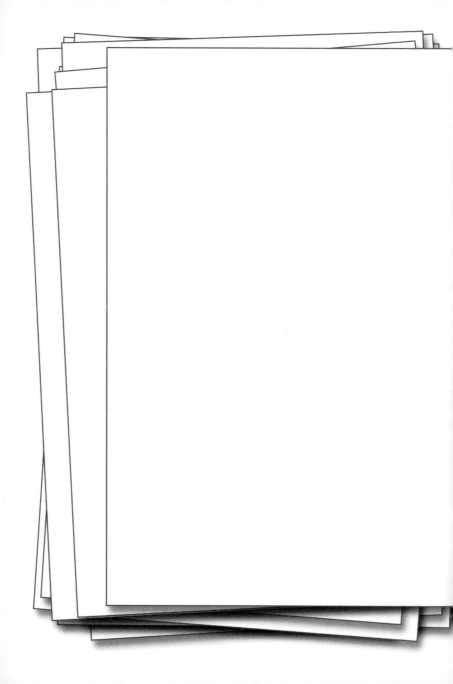

...within a few minutes she will have access to a knife.

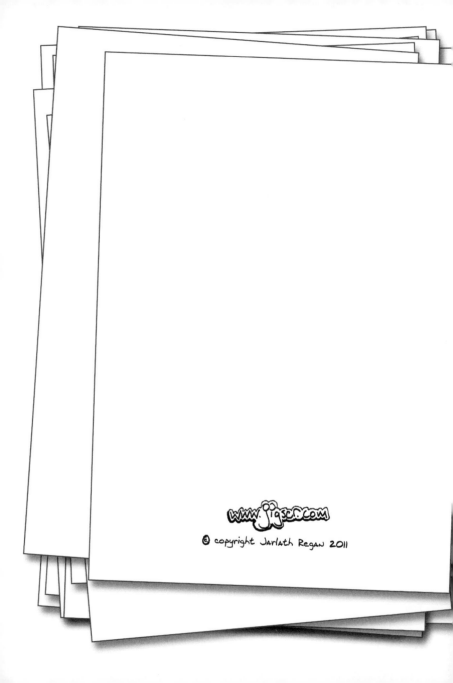

A specially choreographed first
dance might look good
on the night...

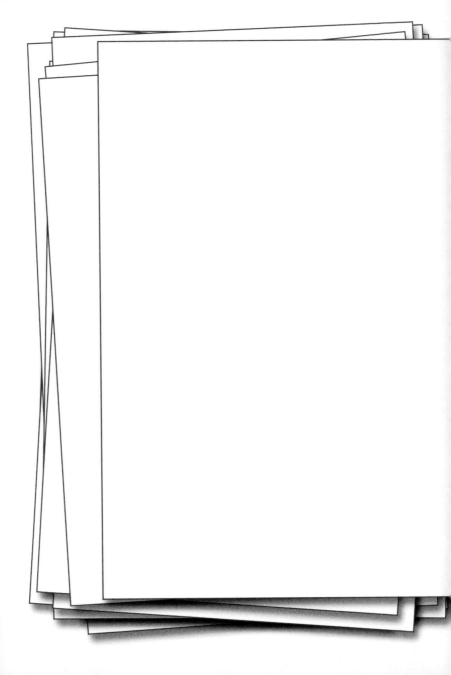

...but is it worth the pain?

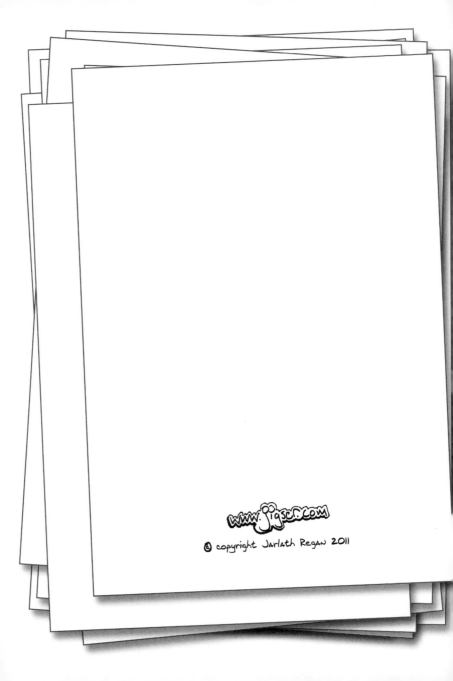

Give your guests a gift they'll
remember...

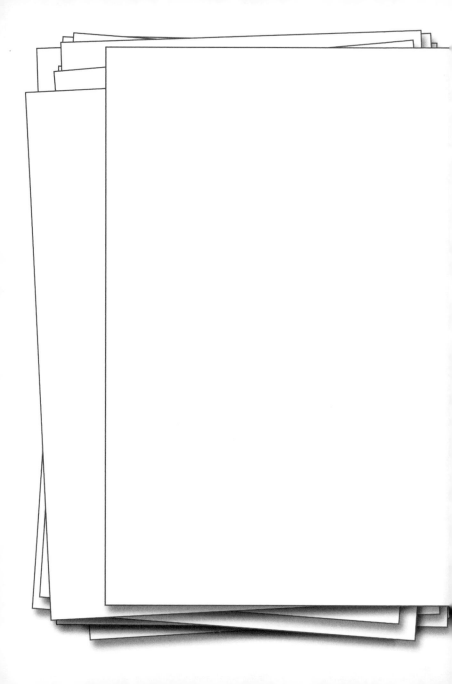

Unexpectedly punch an elderly relative in the face.

Let one of the
groomsmen take care of
the drunken uncle...

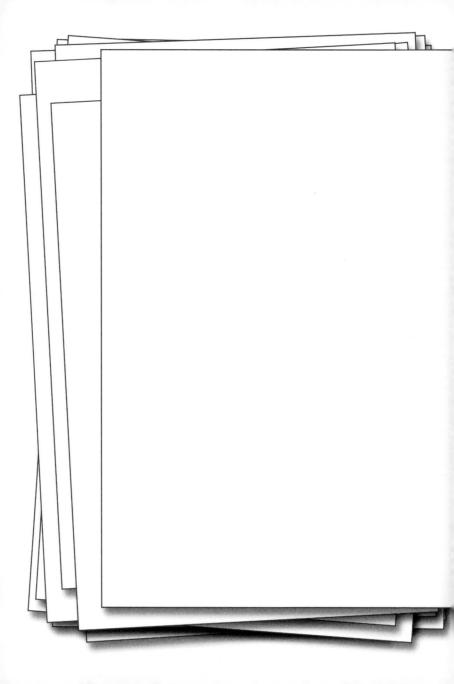

Don't take matters into your own hands.

Chapter 5:
The Wedding Night

Never to be referred to
ever again.

If the wedding ceremony is the
icing on the wedding cake that
is your relationship...

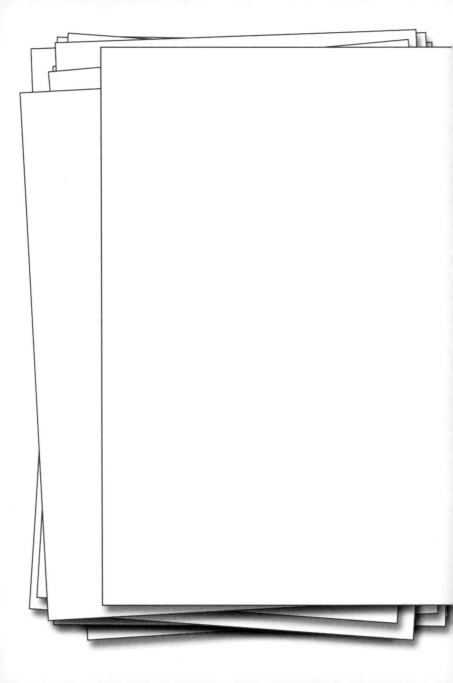

...the wedding-night sex is often
the disappointingly stodgy
interior.

Assume she is wearing sexy
underwear...

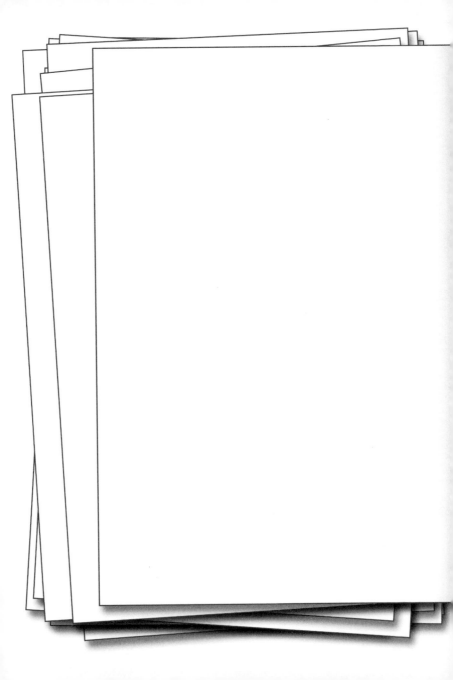

Do not expect it.

WARN your bride that you will
look different on the day...

...and by the evening you may
taste different too.

Didn't bother to work out in
the lead-up to the wedding?

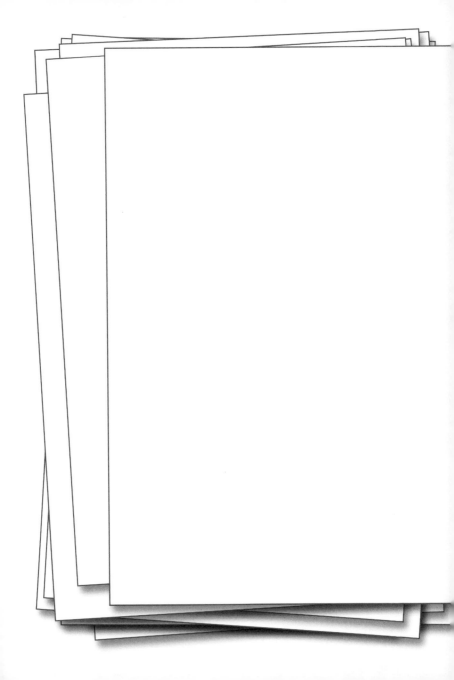

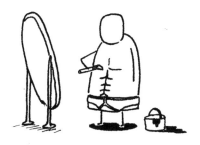

Use body paint to create the
six-pack of her dreams.

It's a little-known fact about
the wedding night...

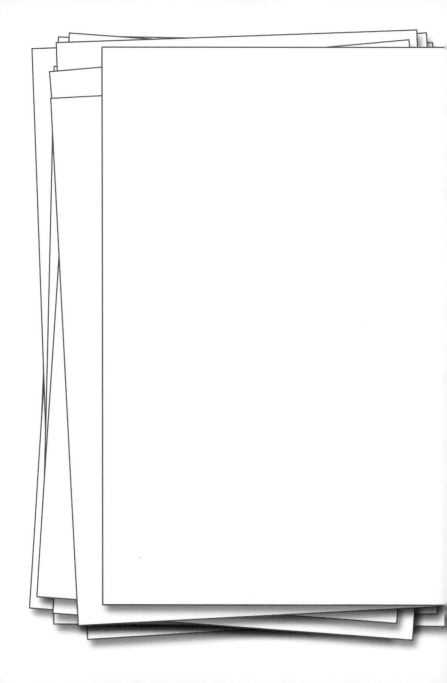

...that most couples don't have sex.

Don't let her delegate too
much to her bridesmaids...

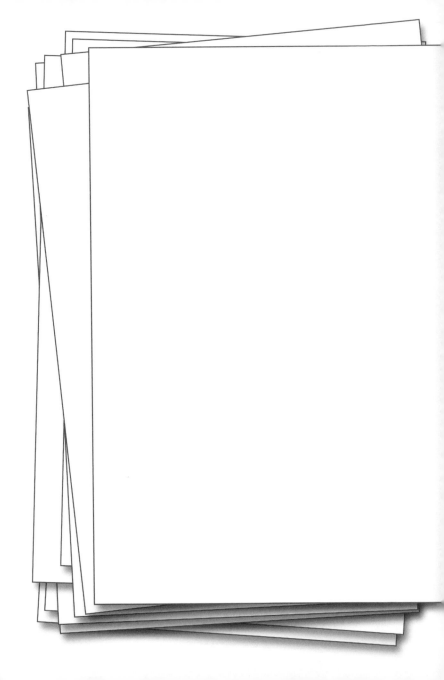

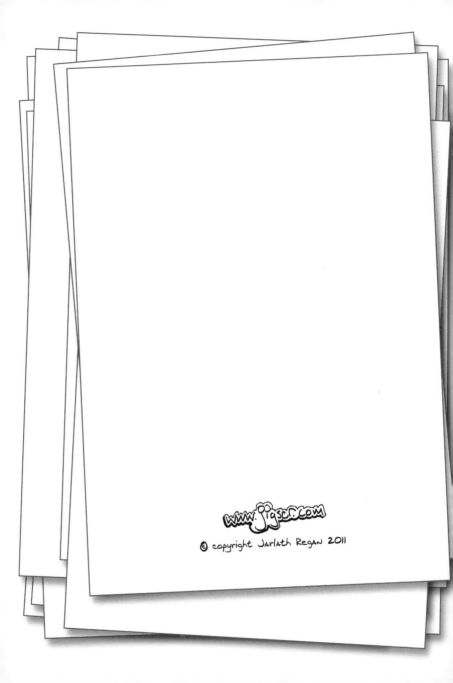

After the stress of the day, her goal might be to achieve unconsciousness as soon as possible...

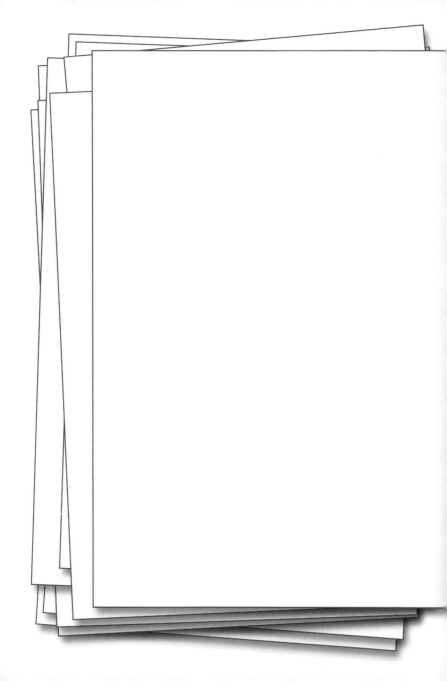

You could let her rest or take advantage of the situation.

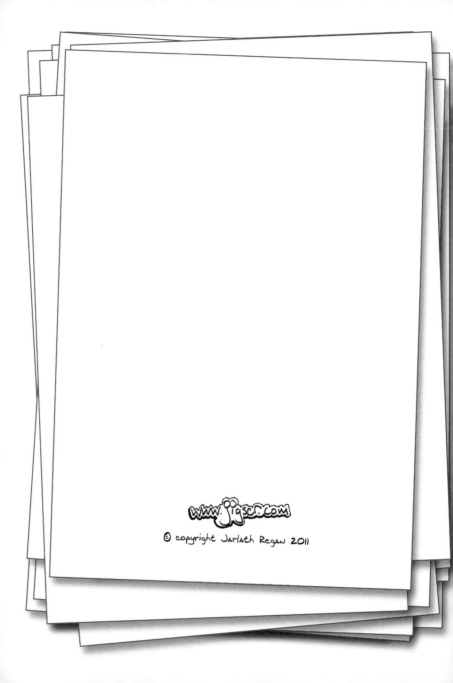

The kinkier the
suggestion...

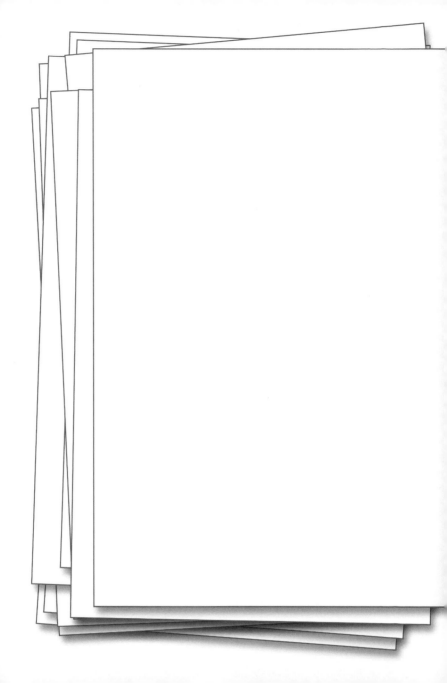

...the less chance it will
happen.

The morning after, when people suggest you should have a child...

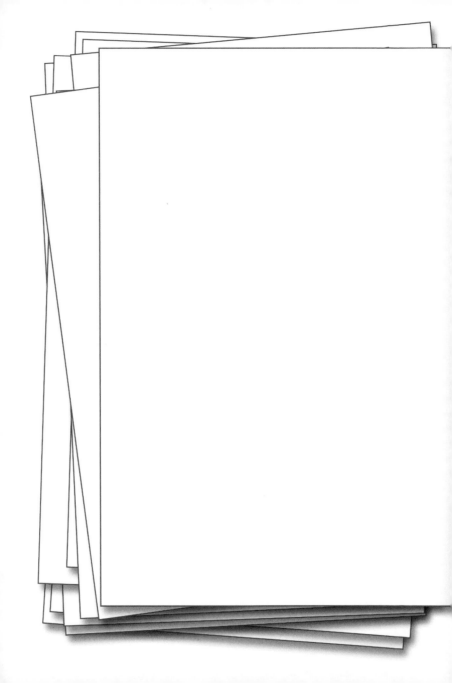

...it's not an invitation to snatch a baby.

Things might get crazy in
the days leading up to the
big day...

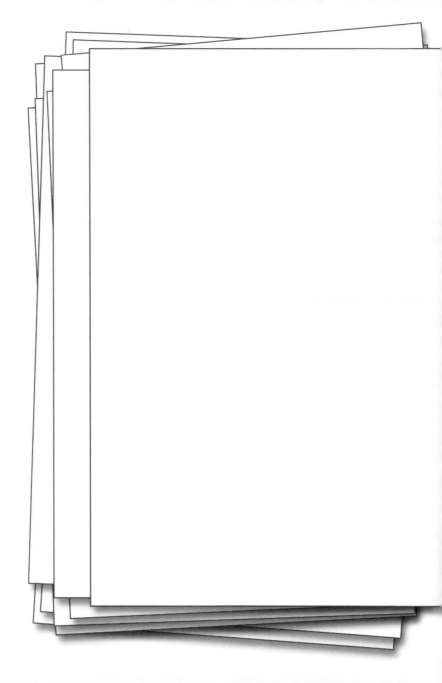

Remember to remind each other
why you are getting married.